# EMI

## AND THE RHINO SCIENTIST

In memory of rhinoceros conservationist Thomas John Foose, 1945–2006

# Mary Kay Carson

With photographs by Tom Uhlman

# EMI
## AND THE RHINO SCIENTIST

HOUGHTON MIFFLIN COMPANY    Boston 2007

The book design is by YAY! Design.
The text is set in Neuzeit.
The maps and graphs are by Jerry Malone.

Library of Congress Cataloging-in-Publication Data

Carson, Mary Kay.
Emi and the rhino scientist
written by Mary Kay Carson ; photographs by Tom Uhlman.
    p. cm.
ISBN-13: 978-0-618-64639-5 (hardcover)
ISBN-10: 0-618-64639-6 (hardcover)
    1.  Sumatran rhinoceros—Juvenile literature.
    2.  Sumatran rhinoceros—Conservation—Juvenile literature.
    3.  Roth, Terri L.—Juvenile literature.
    I. Title.

QL737.U63C37 2007
599.66'8—dc22

2006034517

Printed in Singapore
TWP 10 9 8 7 6 5 4 3 2 1

Photo credits on page 56.

Researcher devotes study
to Sumatran rhino birth

By John Johnston

A RARITY: Sumatran rhino birth

Sumatran rhinoceros is born at Cincinnati

captivity birth
112 years ago

**Emi and her year-old son, Andalas, enjoy some quality mud time.**

# CONTENTS

**Emi and her six-week-old daughter, Suci, butt heads during playtime.**

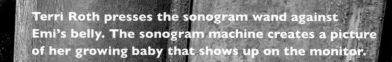
Terri Roth presses the sonogram wand against Emi's belly. The sonogram machine creates a picture of her growing baby that shows up on the monitor.

# AN INSIDE LOOK

**A** group of people crowded around a tall woman with long hair. She was dressed in scrubs, like a surgeon, and stood next to a computer. Everyone moved in for a closer look when the woman pointed to the screen. On it was a fuzzy picture called a sonogram. The blurry black-and-white image was of a baby still inside its mother. It wasn't yet ready to be born.

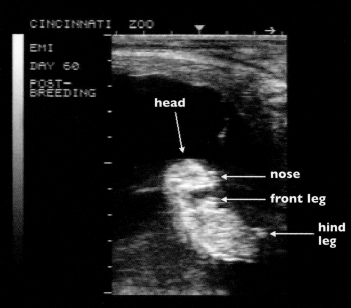

CINCINNATI ZOO
EMI
DAY 60
POST-BREEDING

head
nose
front leg
hind leg

**These are sonogram images of Emi's baby. Its head, nose, rump, and legs are labeled. Can you make them out?**

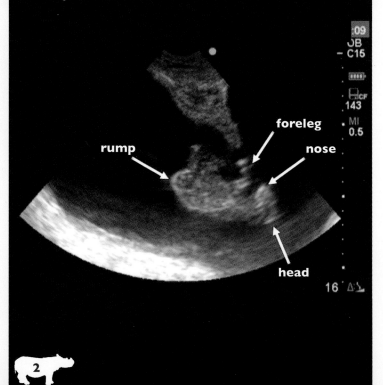

foreleg
nose
rump
head

:09
JB
C15
CF
143
MI
0.5

16

2

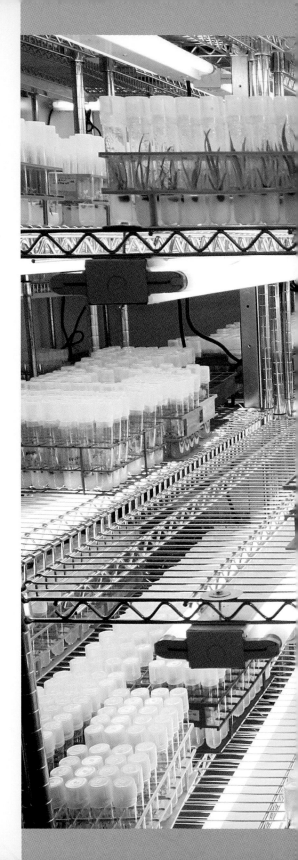

It was hard to spot the baby in the fuzzy sonogram. But the woman, Terri Roth, was patient with her guests. She smiled and pointed out the baby's head on the screen. Then Terri pointed to an ear, the baby's huge nose, and a front foot. A front foot? This baby wasn't human. It was a rhinoceros. The rhino baby's mother was Emi (EHM-mee). It was July of 2000, and Emi was only a few months pregnant; she had more than a year left to go. Rhino mothers give birth to one calf after sixteen months of pregnancy. Emi had been pregnant five times before, though she'd never had a calf—all five of those pregnancies had ended in miscarriage. "I felt sick to my stomach each time," said Terri.

Terri Roth had been trying to help Emi and her mate, Ipuh (EE-poo), have a calf for nearly four years. As an expert in endangered species reproduction, she has the job of breeding rare animals. Terri's the director of CREW, which stands for the Center for Conservation and Research of Endangered Wildlife, at the Cincinnati Zoo. Endangered wildlife are animals and plants in danger of becoming extinct. An extinct animal is one that no longer exists on earth, and won't ever again. Extinction is forever. CREW works to save endangered wildlife from becoming extinct.

All kinds of plants and plant tissues are grown in this CREW laboratory.

CREW scientists study endangered animals, such as ocelots and manatees, to find out why they're disappearing. CREW also supports wildlife reserves so animals such as cheetahs and okapis have a home safe from hunters. And CREW collects tissue from rare plants, such as Florida papaws, so they can be grown elsewhere. A big part of CREW's work is breeding endangered animals at the Cincinnati Zoo. All kinds of rare creatures have been born there—from gorillas and monkeys to elephants, fishing cats, and frogs. "Zoos can play a big role," says Terri. "We are always breeding animals with the idea of someday returning them to their natural environment."

As director, Terri Roth keeps all of CREW's projects on track. "This job suits me so well partly because I love the animals," Terri says. She learned to love animals growing up in rural California. As a kid, Terri caught lots of snakes, toads, and lizards in nearby fields. "I had a horse. We raised a bottle calf, rabbits, and parakeets—and had guinea pigs," she remembers. Terri got started breeding animals as a kid in 4-H, an agricultural youth club. She raised lambs. "I took them to the fair, showed them, and sold them."

When she was growing up, Terri visited her grandparents every summer in Southern

**Young Terri with one of the lambs she raised.**

A herd of rhino statues from around the world keeps Terri company while she works in her office. Terri is the vice president of Conservation, Science & Living Collections at the Cincinnati Zoo and Botanical Garden, as well as the director of CREW.

**Emi happily munches on leaves while being petted by Terri in the rhino's indoor stall.**

California. "We'd always go to the San Diego Zoo," says Terri. And she loved seeing the animals there. What did Terri think she wanted to be when she grew up? "I was either going to work in a zoo or I was going to be a jockey," she says with a laugh. She soon grew too tall to ride racehorses for a living, but the dream of working with zoo animals came true.

Besides working with animals, the other part of being CREW's director that suits Terri so well is the science: "I really love the challenge of science," she says. Terri studied animal science in college. "School wasn't always easy," she admits. It seemed as though she had to study a lot more than her friends did. It was a great teacher who got her interested in the science of animal breeding. "I really liked breeding animals because that's what I did with my lambs," explains Terri. She spent years studying high-tech ways to help breed horses. Then she worked on breeding rare cheetahs and snow leopards at the National Zoo in Washington, D.C. By the time Terri Roth came to CREW, she was an expert at breeding endangered animals like Emi, the struggling rhino mom.

Back in the room full of sonogram watchers, everyone was eyeing the unborn

**Every year there are fewer Sumatran rhinos. Twenty years ago there were one thousand. Poaching and loss of habitat have reduced their numbers to around three hundred.**

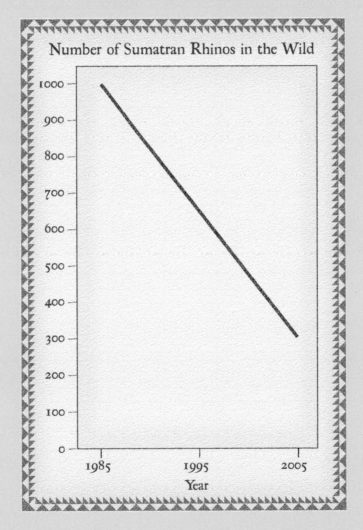

Number of Sumatran Rhinos in the Wild

calf on the computer screen. It squirmed a bit inside its mother. Terri said that Emi's growing baby looks healthy. Would this calf be the one that makes it? Had Terri finally figured out how to help Emi become a mother? Would Emi's baby be born?

Lots of people hoped so. The unborn calf wasn't just any rhino. It was a very rare Sumatran rhino. Sumatran rhinos like Emi are the earth's smallest rhinoceros. These hairy rhinos from Asia are among the most endangered mammals in the world. Over the past fifteen years, hunters have killed half of the world's Sumatran rhinos. These illegal hunters, called poachers, kill Sumatrans for their valuable horns. Only three hundred or so Sumatran rhinos remain in the shrinking forests of Southeast Asia.

Sumatran rhinos could easily go extinct, so every new Sumatran rhino born is precious. No one who squinted at Emi's sonogram was alive when the last Sumatran rhino was born in a zoo; it happened more than one hundred years ago. "Sumatran rhinos are one of the most difficult species to breed and maintain in captivity," says Terri Roth. Emi still had a long way to go. But if her baby was born, it wouldn't just make Terri happy. It'd make history.

Thousands of years ago woolly rhinos like these roamed the grasslands and snowy tundras of Europe and Asia. Sumatran rhinos are their direct descendants, and the last living members of the woolly rhino family.

# MEET THE PARENTS

**R**hinoceroses have roamed the earth for a long time—fifty million years. That's two hundred times longer than humans. You might not recognize an ancient prehistoric rhino if you saw one. Many millions of years ago, rhinos came in all sorts of shapes and sizes. There were long-legged rhinos that looked like horses and gigantic treetop-munching rhinos bigger than elephants. The woolly rhino was a fur-covered "woolly mammoth-style" rhino with two massive horns. There were even rhinos without horns. Ancient rhinos lived in the cold forests and grasslands of North America and Europe, as well as Africa and Asia.

Modern rhinos—the kind living today—have been around a long time themselves. Scientists have found thirty-million-year-old fossils of hairy Sumatran rhinos, like Emi. That means that Sumatran rhinos have been on earth longer than any other living mammal. They go halfway back to the time when dinosaurs lived. Rhinos have a long, proud history on our planet. Their future is less certain.

## Wild Rhinos

"There are five species of rhinos today," explains Terri. Black rhinos and white rhinos live in Africa. Indian, Sumatran, and Javan rhinos live in Asia. The five kinds of rhinos vary some in size, number of horns, what they eat, and where they live. But all modern rhinos are more alike than different. Everybody recognizes a rhino when they see one. How would you describe a rhino?

You'd probably start with size. "Rhinos are really big animals," says Terri. Only elephants are bigger land animals. Rhinoceroses are built low to the ground. Their wide bodies are propped up on powerful short, thick legs that end in three-toed hooves. Rhinos have thick necks with giant heads and one or two horns. A rhino may look like a slow-moving tank as it lumbers around, but don't be fooled. "Rhinos can move quickly," says Terri. They can whip around in an instant and run as fast

as deer. Rhinos share speed with their close relative the horse.

Like horses, rhinos are plant-eating herbivores. The kinds of plants a rhino eats depends on where it lives. White rhinos live in small herds on Africa's grasslands, called savannahs. They are grazers, mowing down grass with wide mouths that hang low to the ground. Shady tropical forests where Sumatran and Javan rhinos live don't have grass. "These rhinos mostly eat leaves from trees and bushes," says Terri. Africa's black rhinos are browsers, too. They have a special pointy

top lip that's good at grabbing leaves.

Rhinos are covered in thick gray or brown skin that's mostly bare. Most rhinos just have a bit of hair around the ears and eyes—and a tail tuft. Rhino skin, or hide, looks tough, but their skin is actually quite sensitive. Sunburn, bug bites, and thorn scratches irritate a rhino's hide. That's why rhinoceroses love to get dirty. Lying in mud, or wallowing, is like a beauty treatment for rhinos. The mud acts as sunscreen, moisturizing lotion, and bug repellent. Wallowing in mud also helps keep rhinos cool during long hot afternoons. If there's no mud around, rolling

**Rhinos are quick and agile. Black rhinos like this one can run as fast as thirty miles (forty-five kilometers) an hour.**

# Where Rhinos Live Today

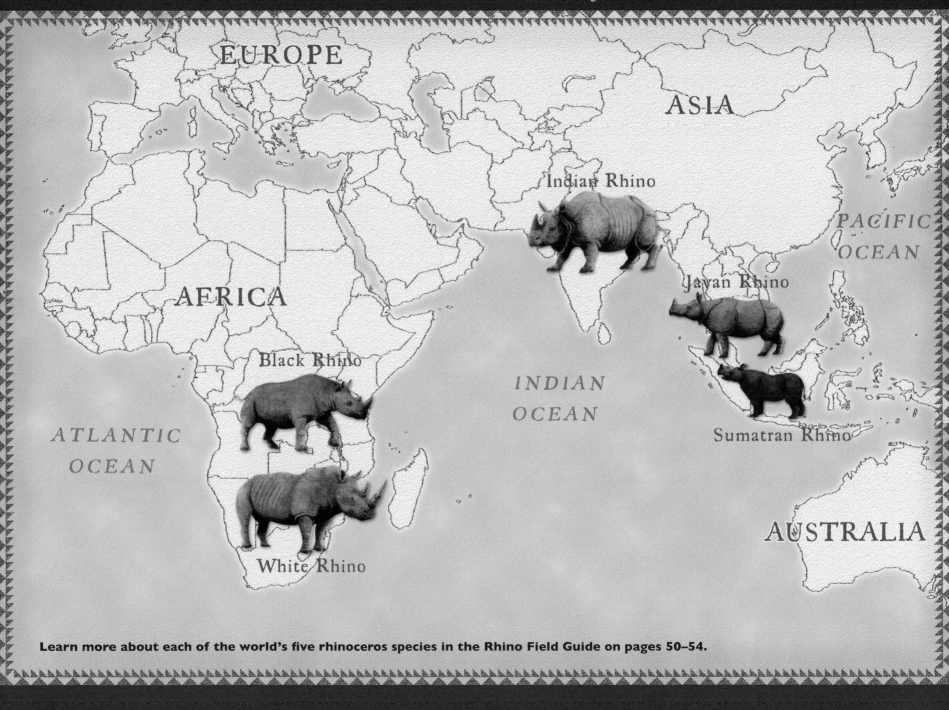

EUROPE

ASIA

PACIFIC
OCEAN

Indian Rhino

Javan Rhino

AFRICA

Black Rhino

Sumatran Rhino

ATLANTIC
OCEAN

INDIAN
OCEAN

White Rhino

AUSTRALIA

Learn more about each of the world's five rhinoceros species in the Rhino Field Guide on pages 50–54.

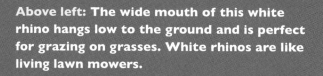

**Above left:** The wide mouth of this white rhino hangs low to the ground and is perfect for grazing on grasses. White rhinos are like living lawn mowers.

**Above:** Sumatran rhinos are browsers and need to eat lots of fresh tropical leaves to stay healthy. Branches full of fig leaves like these are flown in from California twice a month to feed Cincinnati's Sumatran rhinos.

**Above right:** This black rhino's pointy top lip can easily grab and pull off leaves to snack on.

**Left:** A bird looks for tasty insects on the back of an Indian rhino. Indian rhino skin hangs in folds, giving them an armored look.

**Right:** Emi's mate, Ipuh, loves his wallow. It's where he spends most of his time when outside. Besides feeling good, the mud keeps his skin healthy.

in dust will do. Wild rhinos almost always have a layer of dried mud or dirt on them. So what color is a rhino, really? Usually the color of the local dirt.

Rhinos live a long time—up to fifty years. Most of that long life is spent roaming through the forest or savannah, eating leaves or grass. "Rhinos don't have good eyesight," says Terri. They depend more on their sense of smell and their excellent hearing. Rhinos can pinpoint the direction of sounds from very far away. What sound does a rhino itself make? You'd be surprised. Black rhinos are especially chatty. They can growl like a lion, trumpet like an elephant, and squeak like a door. All rhinos snort, huff, squeak, and make other noises to communicate with one another.

Rhinos are famous for their horns. *Rhinoceros* means "nose horn" in Greek, after all. Both kinds of African rhinos have two horns, and so do Sumatrans. Indian and Javan rhinos have only one horn. Rhino horns aren't like bony cow or sheep horns. They are made of keratin, the same tough, stringy stuff in claws, hooves, nails, fur, and hair. Like your fingernails, rhino horns are always growing. If a rhino's horn chips or breaks off it doesn't hurt, and the horn grows back. It's like breaking a fingernail.

Defense is the main job of the horns on African rhinos. Not even lions want to tangle

This Indian rhino is busy listening. Like all rhinos, it can move each ear independently to better follow the direction of sounds.

Like those of all Sumatran rhinos, Emi's two horns are short. The back horn is especially stubby.

with adult rhino horns. However, Sumatran, Javan, and Indian rhinos don't use their horns in battle; their weapons are large, long, pointy canine teeth. "Opponents slash at each other," explains Terri. All rhinos use their horns as tools. They can use their powerful horns to dig up roots, break off branches to get to the tasty leaves, and even uproot small trees.

## Horn Trouble

Rhinos' famous horns have caused them a lot of trouble with poachers. "Rhino horn is very valuable," says Terri. One good-size rhino horn can sell for as much as $50,000. Why? Ground-up rhino horn is a prized medicine in some Asian countries. Rhino horn has been used in traditional Chinese medicine for

This adult black rhino has few natural predators. These male lions are no match for the rhino's powerful horns.

**Kenya's growing capital city comes right up to the edge of Nairobi National Park. Black rhinos currently live in the park, but space for wildlife is shrinking as the city expands.**

more than a thousand years to treat fever and other illnesses. Rhino horn is also prized by carvers of ceremonial dagger handles in the Middle Eastern country of Yemen. Between 1970 and 1987 more than one hundred tons of rhino horn were bought and sold around the world. That's at least 40,000 dead rhinos' worth of horn. A rhino isn't going to give up its horn without a fight, so poachers kill them before cutting off the horns. Buying and selling rhino horn is now illegal, but poaching rhinos for their pricey horns still goes on. Rhino poachers risk arrest because a single rhino horn sells for more money than most of the people in their underdeveloped countries earn in an entire year. Greed fuels the rhino horn trade, but it's often desperate poverty that creates poachers.

When rhinos disappear from a forest or grassland, it changes the ecosystem. An ecosystem is all the living things in an area and their environment. Rhinos help shape the landscape of their environment by eating branches, creating trails, and digging wallows. Rhinos also spread the seeds of the fruits and nuts they eat—and are walking fertilizers. One rhino poops out about sixty pounds (twenty-seven kilograms) of dung a day. Rhinos help keep an ecosystem healthy for hundreds of birds, bugs, and other creatures.

It takes a lot of land to grow all the grass, leaves, or other plants large rhinos need to survive. Losing habitat—the land, water, and plants that animals need to live—is the other big problem rhinos have besides poachers. As more and more rhino habitat is taken over by towns and farms, there is less room for rhinos to live. Since 1970 the world population of rhinos has decreased by about 90 percent. That means that nine out of every ten rhinos are gone. That's bad news for rhinos—and the ecosystems they leave behind.

Fewer than 18,000 rhinos are left on earth today. That's the population of one small town. More than 11,000 (about two-thirds) of all the world's remaining rhinos are white rhinos. Years of protection and work by conservationists have brought back southern Africa's white rhinos. "White rhinos have been downlisted to threatened because they've made such a comeback," says Terri. Black,

Javan, Sumatran, and Indian rhino have it much worse. These four rhino species are critically endangered. That means they're extremely close to going extinct. There are probably more kids in your school than there are Sumatran and Javan rhinos in the whole world.

## Emi and Ipuh's Story

Emi and her mate, Ipuh, know firsthand the trouble rhinos are in. Both were lucky to survive as long as they did in the wild. In 1991, Emi was a young rhino living alone in the forests of Sumatra. She was orphaned—a poacher likely killed her mother. "Sumatran rhino calves usually stay with their mothers for one and a half to two years," explains Terri Roth. (Rhino fathers don't take part in caring for calves.) More and more poachers were making their way into Emi's forest in 1991, and loggers were building more and more roads through the forest. Each logging truck full of trees carried another piece of Emi's home away. These new roads also made it easier for poachers to find rhinos.

Conservationists found Emi in a pit trap. They'd dug the pit traps to capture rhinos before their forest was totally cut down. The conservationists hoped that the captured rhinos could be part of a captive breeding program. If conservationists can successfully breed captive Sumatran rhinos, there will still be some left, even if all the wild Sumatran rhinos die out. Captive-born Sumatran rhinos could then perhaps someday be moved back to protected forests.

Emi didn't panic when the trappers found her in the pit, even though she wasn't used to people. Emi calmly snacked on leafy branches handed to her. It took eight days for Emi to travel from Sumatra to America. A truck took her to the coast and a ferry carried her to the Indonesian city of Jakarta. Next was a long airplane ride to California. Easygoing Emi quickly settled into her new home at the Los Angeles Zoo. The young rhino happily squeaked as she pushed around a large ball and waded in her pool.

Meanwhile, another Sumatran rhino arrived in America from Sumatra. Conservationists had also caught an adult male rhino named Ipuh in a shrinking forest. Trappers loaded up Ipuh in a wooden crate and floated him across a river on a raft. Then a truck eventually took him to an airplane bound for America. In late 1991 Ipuh

**Terri looks over a pile of confiscated poachers' snares and a few rhino bones while visiting Indonesia. Park rangers collect the snares in the forests.**

**Ipuh in his outdoor exhibit at the Cincinnati Zoo, where he's lived since 1991.**

moved into a brand-new Sumatran rhino exhibit at the Cincinnati Zoo. "Emi and Ipuh were captured in an area that was about to be logged," explains Terri, "so these are animals that would have been doomed." Since Emi's and Ipuh's capture, poachers have killed around four hundred Sumatran rhinos. Illegal hunting has reduced the wild population to less than half of what it was fifteen years ago. Living in a zoo isn't the same as roaming the forests of Sumatra, but Emi and Ipuh were alive and safe.

In Los Angeles, Emi was growing up fast. Within a few years zoo workers began wondering if Emi was ready to be a mother. Unfortunately, none of the captive rhinos living in Indonesia or Malaysia had given birth. Not a single calf. And no one was sure why. In fact, at the time of Emi's capture in 1991, a Sumatran rhino hadn't bred and given birth to a calf in captivity anywhere since 1889. CREW scientists at the Cincinnati Zoo wanted to see if they could solve the captive Sumatran rhino breeding mystery. So in 1995 Emi moved to Cincinnati to be with Ipuh. Everyone hoped the two rhinos would get along. Ipuh was the only male Sumatran rhino in the entire United States. No one had higher hopes than CREW's new director. Terri Roth believed Emi and Ipuh could help save their species from extinction. All she had to do was figure out how to help the hefty, hairy couple become parents.

**Emi in her outdoor exhibit at the Cincinnati Zoo, where she's lived since 1995.**

Ipuh takes it easy and enjoys a mud bath, and cools off in his pool.

# PUTTING
# THE PIECES
# TOGETHER

**I**puh wanted to go to the pool. The big male rhino had finished his breakfast of leafy branches and veggies in his indoor stall. It was morning, but it was already hot and sticky on that summer day in Cincinnati in 1997. The zookeeper opened the gate to the outdoor rhino yard. Ipuh marched across the dusty yard surrounded by rock walls and headed straight for the water. The 1,600-pound (726-kilogram) rhino eased down into the small concrete pool. Ahhhh.

Wild Sumatran rhinos spend their lives alone, searching for food in forests and relaxing in mud. Ipuh lives a solitary life at the zoo, too—usually. This day was going to be different. Ipuh was getting a visitor. The gate opened again. Another rhino trotted out into the yard—a female! Emi's entrance wasn't exciting enough to get Ipuh out of his pool that first day. But it was the start of something amazing.

"Emi is a very curious rhino," says Terri. "She'd go over to Ipuh as if asking, 'Who are you?'" remembers Terri. "It was really cool." It could have been really *un*cool. Sumatran rhinos often fight when they're put together. In the wild, a rhino can just run away from a fight if it wants. In captivity there's usually not enough space for a female to safely get away from an aggressive male. "We had zoo volunteer observers watching them the entire time with radios," says Terri. "So if anything happened, they could call the keepers." Fortunately, Ipuh didn't charge or attack Emi. The first half-hour visit was peaceful.

## Getting from A to B

Putting Ipuh and Emi together like this was not Plan A. Terri wanted to put the couple together only at the exact time when Emi could get pregnant. Female mammals, including rhinos, have a reproductive cycle that

**Terri looks over some of Emi's hormone test results at the CREW laboratory.**

prepares them for pregnancy. An important part of this cycle is ovulation, when an egg inside the female is sent toward the womb. If the traveling egg meets up with sperm from the male, settles into the womb, and starts growing into a baby, the female's pregnant.

A male rhino welcomes a female rhino that's about to ovulate. He wants to father offspring, so he doesn't try to fight her. Figuring out the timing of Emi's reproductive cycle wasn't easy. Terri had already spent the winter and spring studying Emi—with no luck. How can you tell when a rhino is ovulating? One way is to look inside and see if an egg is on the move, which a sonogram can show. Another way is to test her blood to see if the hormones have changed.

So how do you get blood from a big wild animal? Terri says rhinos are easier to work with than you might think. "Because the rhino is what it is, it doesn't have a lot of fear of us," Terri explains. Flighty gazelles or fierce predators like tigers are far trickier. Vets must anesthetize a sick tiger with drugs before examining it. An anesthetized animal—or person—can't feel anything and is in a deep sleep. Anesthesia is an important tool for both vets and surgeons. It's usually safe, but it isn't risk-free. Powerful anesthesia drugs sometimes make animals and people sick, and can even accidentally kill them. Anesthetizing

Terri watches Emi walking into her chute as the scientist gets ready to do a sonogram. Emi knows she'll be getting treats soon, so she doesn't mind.

a rhino is a lot of work, too. It takes a team of vets to do it safely.

Instead of being anesthetized, many rhinos can be trained to willingly put up with medical exams. How? By using treats. It all starts with tempting a rhino to walk into a narrow chute made of thick bars. There are bananas, apples, or other snacks inside. Once the chute's gate is closed, Terri carefully takes blood or uses the sonogram machine while the rhino happily munches away. "The rhinos have to volunteer to do it," says Terri. If a rhino won't walk into the chute, then the tests don't happen. "But Emi is a trouper," says Terri. "She always cooperates with us." Chute training means that Terri can quickly and safely check Emi as often as she needs, without the extra work and worry of anesthesia. Plus, working with an undrugged, alert animal is more fun. "For those of us who love animals, it's kind of neat, because rhinos have their own personalities," says Terri. "You get to know them when they're awake."

Though Emi was a model patient, Terri was still in the dark about the young rhino's reproductive cycle. With other kinds of rhinos Terri had been able to easily learn how long a female's reproductive cycle is. Terri simply watched for ovulation, counting the days from one ovulation until the next. That number of days told Terri how long the rhino's cycle is and when exactly is the best time for breeding.

Unfortunately, Emi wasn't showing any normal signs of ovulating. The sonogram never showed

19

Spending time with Emi is always fun for Terri.

eggs releasing. And the hormones in Emi's blood didn't hint at ovulation either. Could there be something wrong with Emi? Was Emi never ovulating for some reason? This wasn't how it worked with other kinds of rhinos. Was Terri not looking for the right clues? Maybe Sumatran rhinos weren't like other rhinos. "It was really hard for me to figure out what was going on with her," says Terri. "Basically the data were a mess." By summer Terri was ready to try Plan B.

## Not Love at First Sight

Terri hoped that putting the rhino couple together every day would solve the ovulation mystery. She'd know when Emi was ovulating because the rhinos should naturally breed then. All she had to do was wait and watch. Unfortunately, Plan B didn't seem to be working either. At least, not at first. Ipuh didn't attack Emi when she arrived in his yard every morning, but he didn't seem interested in mating with her either. Ipuh stayed sunk down in his pool while each day Emi dared to come a little bit closer to him.

After forty-two days of friendly visits, Ipuh suddenly got interested. "Ipuh just came right out of the pool, started following Emi around the yard, and started trying to mount her," says Terri. "They went through this attempted breeding all day. We kept them

**Ipuh mounts Emi during mating.**

together and kept watching them all night long." After it was over, Terri examined Emi. The rhino's body had released an egg—she'd ovulated. And that's when Terri cracked the case. Emi had never ovulated before because she'd never mated before. *Wow!* thought Terri, *Emi's an induced ovulator.*

There are some kinds of mammals that release eggs only after breeding—cats and rabbits, for example. They're called induced ovulators. Mating induces, or causes, them to ovulate. No eggs are released until they start breeding. But rhinos aren't known to be induced ovulators—at least, not any rhinos anyone had studied before. "It's only Sumatran rhinos," explains Terri. CREW scientist Terri Roth had made a big discovery. There was nothing wrong with Emi. Sumatran rhinos were just different. "I was starting to put the pieces together," Terri said.

A few weeks later Ipuh and Emi mated again. And this time Emi got pregnant. The news spread around the world that a captive Sumatran rhino was finally pregnant. Unfortunately, only six weeks into the pregnancy, something went wrong. Emi miscarried. While Terri was disappointed, she felt sure that the rhino could get pregnant again. She'd already solved the mystery of Emi's cycle. The scientist could now predict the exact twenty-four-hour period when Emi could get

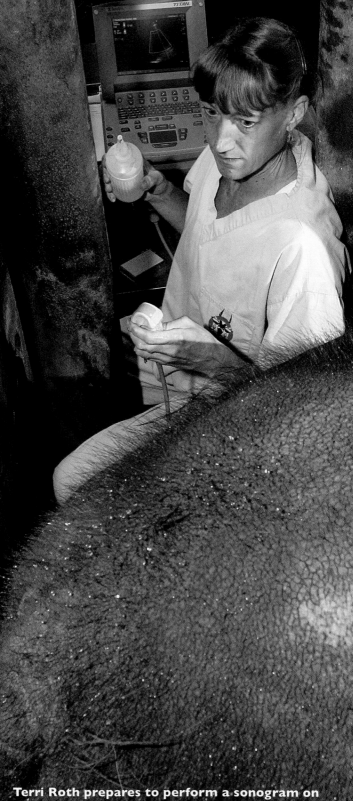

**Terri Roth prepares to perform a sonogram on pregnant Emi while the rhino stands in her chute.**

pregnant. Terri sonogrammed Emi to see if she was getting ready to release an egg and checked Emi's blood for the telltale hormone levels. When the time was right, Emi and Ipuh were put together. The couple mated, and sure enough, Emi got pregnant again. Sadly, Emi lost this second pregnancy early on, too. And then it happened again—and again.

Over three years Emi got pregnant five times and lost all five pregnancies within the first three months. Even worse, no one knew *why* Emi couldn't stay pregnant. Was Emi not getting something in captivity that wild Sumatrans had? Figuring out what wild animals need to breed in captivity is tricky. Zoos do their best to recreate a natural environment for their animals and meet their needs. Identifying those needs is the tough part. Flamingos need to live in flocks to breed, for example. And many frogs need the weather to match their breeding season in the wild before mating. Cincinnati isn't Sumatra, but Emi seemed healthy and content. Why wasn't Emi staying pregnant?

These were hard years for everyone trying to help Sumatran rhinos at the Cincinnati Zoo, and around the world. It was Terri Roth who examined Emi, so Terri was always the first to find out when Emi had another miscarriage. Telling everyone the bad news was tough. "They'd want answers," says

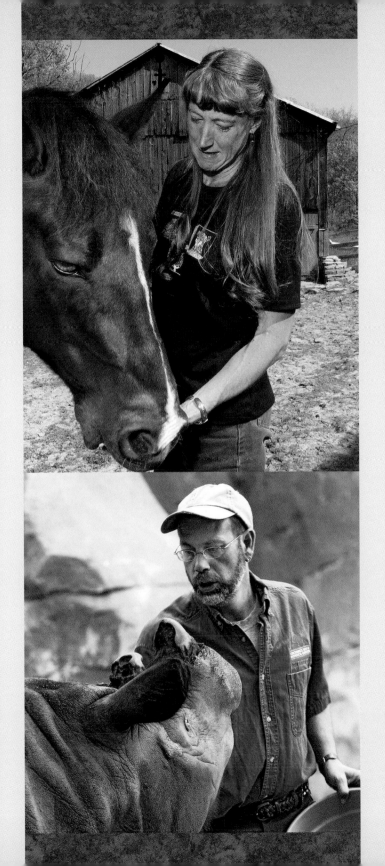

**Terri gives her horse, Turbo, a snack. Terri got the idea of giving a hormone supplement to Emi from her experience with horses.**

Terri. "And often I didn't have them." What was wrong? Why was Emi losing the pregnancies? How could Terri help Emi have a calf?

## Horse Sense

Terri Roth started thinking about horses. Rhinos are close relatives of horses', after all. Terri grew up with horses and has a horse named Turbo on her Kentucky farm now. Terri had also worked on high-tech horse breeding in college, where she'd learned a lot about new techniques and drugs used to help horses get pregnant and deliver healthy foals. Terri knew that horse vets sometimes give extra hormones to mares that are losing pregnancies. Horses—and rhinos—naturally have a hormone called progesterone in their bodies. Drug companies also make artificial horse progesterone that can be given to mares as a supplement.

"There are no how-to books on how to breed an endangered species," explains Terri. "Sometimes you just have to try something and see if it works." Getting a progesterone supplement sometimes helps a horse stay pregnant. Could it do the same for Emi? When Emi got pregnant for the sixth time in June of 2000 (see the timeline on page 26), a decision was made. The mother rhino would get a daily dose of artificial horse hormone. Terri had no idea if it'd help.

Luckily for zookeeper Paul Reinhart, Emi cheerfully took her hormone supplement each day—with a treat. The hormone supplement is liquid, so Paul simply soaked slices of bread with it. "Every morning, she'd be waiting, looking for her bread. It was amazing," says Terri. Paul explains, "I'd just stand here and put a little bit on a piece of bread and hand-feed it to her." By the time the stack of bread was gone, so was the day's dose.

One hundred days of hormone-soaked bread passed by with Emi still pregnant. Terri kept examining Emi regularly, checking on her growing baby. Rhino pregnancies last about sixteen months. After eight long months, the mother-to-be rhino passed the halfway point. CREW decided it was safe to announce Emi's pregnancy to the public. Now people throughout the whole world were holding their breath and waiting. Could this finally be the baby that survived?

On day 465 of her pregnancy, Paul fed Emi her final stack of hormone-soaked bread. Was it the supplement that had kept Emi pregnant for sixty weeks? "We may never know for sure," admits Terri. There's just too much scientists don't know about rhinos—especially rare Sumatran rhinos.

Paul has been a rhino zookeeper for twenty-five years. He's cared for a number of pregnant black rhinos and their calves. Paul was going to make sure Emi's pregnancy was

**Paul feeds Emi some treats.**

as stress-free as possible. "I try to make her happy," says Paul. Emi pretty much ate what she wanted, when she wanted. And she spent as much time out in the yard as she wanted, too. "Emi's spoiled," admits Paul. "But these animals are so rare. Emi and Ipuh can't be replaced, even if you had ten million dollars." Emi's keeper was doing whatever he could to help one more Sumatran rhino be born.

## The Big Day

Emi was feeling cranky. The 475-day pregnant rhino had been moody and irritable for days. She swaggered back and forth across her indoor stall. Her belly was so big, she could only lie down if she flopped over on her side. Paul had even seen Emi's baby turning inside her. "You could see a leg or foot push against the inside of her belly," says Paul. "We knew it was coming. She was pacing so much, and she started spraying urine and was very restless." It was time for Emi to have her calf.

Early the morning of September 13, 2001, everyone was ready. The zoo's vets were there. Horse milk was on hand, just in case Emi wouldn't nurse. Terri Roth had been at the zoo all night, waiting and watching Emi in her stall. Paul showed up around seven in the morning. When Emi saw her keeper walk in, she decided she wanted him to serve her breakfast before giving birth!

After eating breakfast, Emi went back to work. Terri watched as the pregnant rhino paced a bit more, then finally lay down. Emi quickly pushed the calf out of her body and into the world. "Even before he was all the way out, I saw his front legs kicking," said Terri. It was a relief to finally know for sure that Emi's calf was okay.

The newborn rhino was covered in dark wet hair. It was a boy! He lay on the straw-covered floor and shook his head, his big, dark round eyes wide open. Emi was exhausted. The new mother got up and walked away from her calf. Would she know how to care for him—or want to? Emi was an orphan herself, after all. "Nobody had any idea what kind of mother she'd be," remembers Paul. Emi soon walked back toward the little calf still lying on the floor. She lowered her enormous head down to him, and started to lick him all over. She did know what to do. Once Emi had her son cleaned up, she stood close by as he tried to stand for the first time. His short thick legs wobbled and shook with effort. Then he was up. Soon he was standing strong under his mom's belly to nurse.

Terri smiled with relief and happiness as she watched the calf nursing. "It's a little hard to believe he's here," Terri told a newspaper reporter. "I've been working on this for years and years. We've had many disappointments."

Emi's newborn calf is soon standing up on his own.

Emi gets a playful nip from her new son.

Terri says hello to Emi's young calf.

24

Terri watches Emi successfully
giving birth via live video cameras
in the rhino stall.

Seeing Emi and her son together made all the hard work worth it and all the disappointment disappear. Emi and Ipuh were finally parents. And there was one more Sumatran rhino in the world. A check by the vet declared the calf to be a healthy seventy-three-pound (thirty-three-kilogram) baby boy. "It's hard to believe that the calf is thriving and jumping around and is perfect," Terri told the reporter with awe.

News of the first Sumatran rhino born in captivity in more than a hundred years spread quickly. The little rhino's baby picture showed up in newspapers around the globe. A month later, Emi's calf was given a name. Indonesian wildlife officials named him Andalas (ahn-DAHL-us). It's the old name for Sumatra, his mother's island home. To celebrate, the mayor of Cincinnati declared it Sumatran Rhino Day. People crowded along the rock wall that surrounds the rhino yard. Everyone wanted to see Emi's calf romp around and nuzzle his mom. Andalas is the most famous rhino in the world.

**Terri looks in on Emi and month-old Andalas in their outdoor exhibit.**

**Emi presents her new son, Andalas, to the zoo's excited visitors.**

# THE LONG ROAD TO ANDALAS

**FEBRUARY 1997**
- CREW Sumatran rhino breeding project begins.

**SEPTEMBER 1997**
- First successful mating of Emi and Ipuh.
- Discovery that Sumatran rhino is an induced ovulator.

**OCTOBER 1997**
- Emi's first pregnancy lost at day 42.

**1997–2000**
- Ipuh and Emi breed and produce five pregnancies.
- All are lost before the third month.

**JUNE 2000**
- Emi's sixth pregnancy confirmed.
- Emi is started on a daily hormone supplement.

1997          1998          1999          2000

**Andalas plays with his mother's food while exploring his outdoor world.**

**Andalas explores his outdoor exhibit with mom Emi close by.**

**Andalas tastes a dry autumn leaf and licks a bit of dirt. It's all part of learning to be a rhino.**

**JANUARY 2001**
- At day 249, the pregnancy is announced to public.

**SEPTEMBER 3, 2001**
- Emi gets her last dose of hormone supplement.

**SEPTEMBER 13, 2001**
- Emi delivers a male calf after 475 days.

**SEPTEMBER 14, 2001**
- Vet checks Emi's calf, who weighs seventy-three pounds (thirty-three kilograms).

**OCTOBER 2001**
- Calf is named Andalas.
- Emi and Andalas go out into the rhino yard at the zoo and meet the public.

January 2001                     October 2001

Terri gives Emi a nice head-scratching.

# SAVING RHINOS WITH SCIENCE

**A**ndalas's birth gave hope to everyone struggling to save his species. The little calf was one more precious Sumatran rhino on the planet. Terri Roth and the CREW scientists spread the word about how they'd helped Emi give birth. They'd even studied the nutrients in Emi's milk in case they ever needed to make formula for another Sumatran rhino. Everyone would be watching Andalas, learning what Sumatran rhinos need to grow up healthy in captivity.

CREW scientists want others to use what they've learned to help breed captive rhinos of all kinds. "There's a risk of aggression with many rhino species when you put them together," says Terri Roth. "Not just Sumatrans." The way Emi and Ipuh were first put together every day for thirty minutes could help other rhinos mate peacefully, too. And the hormone supplement given to Emi has already been used to help some struggling Indian and black rhino moms give birth.

CREW's motto is Saving Species with Science. "We want to be able to measure our success scientifically," explains Terri. "If you use the scientific method, then you have the data in the end to say whether or not you're successful." Using the scientific method means drawing conclusions only after making careful observations or doing experiments to answer a question or prove a prediction. For example, Terri wanted to breed Emi and Ipuh without the rhinos fighting. She made the prediction that if she put the rhino pair together only when Emi was about to ovulate, there would be no fighting.

"Emi and Ipuh have mated thirty-two times with no serious problems," says Terri. Because she's studied the rhinos and collected data about their peaceful matings, Terri can now conclude that her prediction was right. Using the scientific method proves that

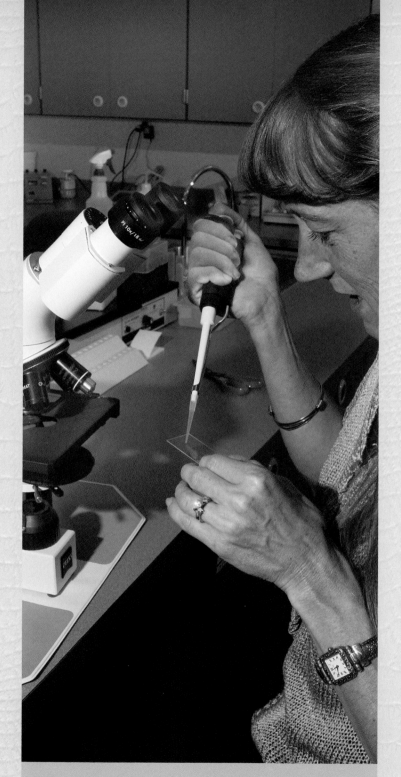

**Terri looks at rhino blood samples under the microscope.**

something works more than once. CREW scientists such as Terri Roth need proof that a breeding technique *consistently* works, as well as *why* it works. That way it can be used again and again—and by others.

CREW scientists are helping breed all four kinds of rhinos that live in captivity: Sumatran, white, black, and Indian rhinos. Why is captive breeding so important? "Most rhinos living in zoos today were born in captivity," says Terri. Zoos work together to breed rhinos—and many other animals—for other zoos. And for endangered animals like rhinos, animals born in captivity can help their species from going extinct.

Zoos also share what they learn about caring for wild animals in captivity. Sumatran rhinos have had health problems in zoos. Emi and Ipuh are the only survivors of seven wild-caught Sumatran rhinos brought to the United States during the 1990s. A few of the seven died of old age, but others had mysterious health problems—even Ipuh. In 1994 Ipuh lost 280 pounds (127 kilograms) over six months. He grew so weak that he stopped moving at all. "Ipuh was twenty-four hours away from dying," says Steve Romo, Ipuh's keeper at the time. Some doubted that Sumatran rhinos could adjust to zoo life, but Steve Romo wondered if maybe Ipuh's diet of hay, alfalfa pellets, and veggies was the problem. Steve's been to Malaysia and Indonesia and knows that these forest rhinos eat lots of leaves. So he asked the San Diego Zoo to ship some leafy fig branches to Cincinnati. As soon as Ipuh smelled the fig leaves he got up for the first time in four days and started eating. With a daily dose of seventy to ninety pounds (thirty-two to forty-one kilograms) of leafy fig branches, Ipuh got better. Leafy branches, called browse, are now fed to all captive Sumatran rhinos.

## Figuring Out What Works

A half dozen huge white animals stroll over grassy hills toward a shining lake. It's a herd of white rhino—in central Ohio! In the Midwest, a wildlife park called the Wilds gives visitors the closest thing to the sight of rhinos in the wild. It's more than just a place to watch giraffes, zebras, and rhinos roam. The Wilds is an important endangered species research and conservation organization. "They've got large expanses of land and a large number of animals," says Terri. This allows scientists at the Wilds to study both the animals and the land around them.

One of the research projects at the Wilds is breeding white rhinos. White rhinos are herd animals that like to live in groups, unlike solitary Sumatrans. One thing that white and Sumatran rhinos do have in common is that they don't always breed easily in captivity. "Many captive white rhino females don't ovulate regularly," says

**Members of the white rhino herd at the Wilds spend much of the year roaming its grasslands.**

Terri. This keeps them from getting pregnant. Part of the problem is having enough room. A white rhino herd needs lots of space. Zoos with limited land can't have a whole herd of huge white rhinos. The 10,000-acre (4,047-hectare) Wilds can. It's a perfect place for white rhinos to roam in a herd and breed naturally.

The Cincinnati Zoo doesn't have the space for white rhinos like the Wilds does. Instead, CREW scientists use the high-tech techniques they're famous for to help the scientists at the Wilds breed rhinos. "We ran hormone levels in their white rhinos to determine which animals were cycling and which animals were not," explains Terri. CREW scientists have also used their sonogram techniques to check for rhino pregnancies at the Wilds. So far, two white rhino calves have been born there.

## High-Tech Help for Indian Rhinos

"Indian rhinos are another rhino that have been difficult for zoos to breed, because they are aggressive," says Terri. Indian rhinos are gigantic. An Indian rhino weighs more than two Sumatrans. When Indian rhinos fight during mating, it can quickly get dangerous. "They race around and it can be pretty scary," says Terri. While zoos might want to use certain Indian rhinos in breeding programs, some are just too aggressive to risk putting together. CREW's answer to the problem is artificial insemination, or AI.

This young white rhino is one of two born at the Wilds.

Nikki, above and at right, is one of two female Indian rhinos at the Cincinnati Zoo. Indian rhinos are big animals, even for rhinos. Nikki weighs about 3,700 pounds (1680 kilograms).

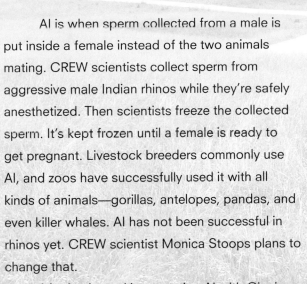

AI is when sperm collected from a male is put inside a female instead of the two animals mating. CREW scientists collect sperm from aggressive male Indian rhinos while they're safely anesthetized. Then scientists freeze the collected sperm. It's kept frozen until a female is ready to get pregnant. Livestock breeders commonly use AI, and zoos have successfully used it with all kinds of animals—gorillas, antelopes, pandas, and even killer whales. AI has not been successful in rhinos yet. CREW scientist Monica Stoops plans to change that.

Monica is working on using AI with Cincinnati's two female Indian rhinos, Chitwan and Nikki. Neither female has had a calf yet. "It's been a challenge," admits Monica. Part of the problem has been getting the female Indian rhinos' reproductive cycles regular enough so that they're ready to be pregnant. Unlike wild animals, zoo animals

**Monica studies a recent sonogram while Chitwan waits for another horse biscuit treat.**

aren't regularly breeding and having offspring. The longer a female rhino goes without having a calf, the harder it becomes for her to get pregnant. Monica's also training the female Indian rhinos to stand in a chute for sonograms and other medical tests, like Emi does. "We hope that Nikki and Chit-wan will be moms soon, too," says Monica.

One advantage of AI is that it's a lot easier to ship frozen sperm to another zoo than to ship a male rhino. Zoos can breed animals that never meet with AI. A mother and father might even live thousands of miles apart. The Frozen Zoo and Garden at CREW is where it's all stored. A room

-196°C -320°F

FROZEN

Terri opens one of the super-cold liquid nitrogen freezer tanks at CREW's Frozen Zoo and takes out a sample tube filled with frozen embryos.

Cincinnati Zoo Center for Reproduction of Endangered Wildlife full of special super-cold freezer tanks holds samples from 60 species of animals and 150 kinds of plants. "There is frozen sperm from rhinos, toads, cheetahs, and penguins," says Terri. There are also frozen gorilla, eland, and ocelot embryos. Other freezers are full of seeds, shoots, and spores from rare plants such as the royal catchfly.

The one rhino species that isn't difficult to breed in captivity is the black rhino. And the Cincinnati Zoo has had lots of success with them. Eighteen black rhino calves have been born there. Most black rhinos breed naturally in captivity, no hormones or AI needed. Just putting a male and female together is all it takes.

While black rhinos are the easiest to breed, they also get sick the most. CREW scientists are working to try to figure out why. Terri says that they've discovered that the black rhino's disease-fighting system isn't as strong as other rhinos'. No one's sure *why* it isn't as strong—yet. So although one piece of the puzzle is solved, another is not. "Working with these endangered species we know so little about, you fail a lot," says Terri. "You have to get some satisfaction out of solving every tiny piece." But the puzzle piece named Andalas wasn't so tiny anymore.

**Below left: This four-month-old black rhino was born at the Cincinnati Zoo in 1995.**

**Below right: A black rhino calf stays close to his mother at the Cincinnati Zoo.**

Andalas sticks close to his mom, Emi, while outside in the Sumatran rhino exhibit.

# ANDALAS

**A**small rhino the size of a stocky dog nuzzles Emi's belly. When the calf turns around, his big round eyes look left and right. His hornless head is covered in long dark hair that looks combed. But Andalas doesn't have hairstyles on his mind right now. It's lunchtime. He goes back to nuzzling Emi, and soon he's happily wagging his tail. Zookeeper Paul Reinhart knows that the small swishing tail means Andalas is happily nursing. As a newborn, Andalas nursed every hour. It's no wonder he put on nearly two and a half pounds (one kilogram) a day.

# GROWS UP

**Mealtime is also lesson time for Andalas and Emi. In he wild, Sumatran calves learn what to eat from their mothers.**

"Emi's been an excellent mother," says Terri Roth. A rhino calf has only his mother to look after him and teach him how to survive. No one knows how young Emi was when she lost her own mother. Could an orphaned rhino make a good mom? "She might not have known what to do—or not had enough milk," says Terri. All the worry was for nothing. Emi is a rhino supermom. Andalas is well fed and tenderly cared for by Emi. "She is such a star," says Paul with pride.

## Rhino Lessons

By the time he's one month old, Andalas already has some teeth. It's time for Emi to teach Andalas what to do with those teeth—eat. As Emi munches

on leaves or hay, she lets her calf nibble on what's sticking out of her own mouth. This teaches Andalas what's safe to eat. In the wild, Sumatran rhinos eat more than one hundred different kinds of plants. They have to learn which plants are good to eat—and which aren't. "Sumatran rhinos have very poor eyesight," explains CREW scientist Bernadette Plair. "This method of eating helps baby rhinos begin learning the proper foods by taste and smell."

Andalas is a quick learner. By the time he's five months old, he's eating fig tree leaves and twigs, orchard grass, pellets of grain, and fruit like apples and bananas. The once 73-pound (33-kilogram) calf is up to 461 pounds (209 kilograms). When Emi and Andalas aren't eating or resting, they play. Chasing each other around the yard and gently butting heads is fun for mom and calf. Playtime also teaches Andalas how to be a rough-and-tumble male rhino.

## Nice Mud, Good Cake

Ten-month-old Andalas is ready to go out. It's a hot July day at the Cincinnati Zoo. But when their gate opens, the calf and his mom are quite surprised. The zoo has remodeled their rhino yard. Emi and Andalas have new low-hanging branches of tasty leaves to nibble on. There's now a waterfall streaming over a rock wall—a perfect rhino shower. Soon Emi and Andalas are sniffing and cir-

**Top: Emi enjoys a waterfall shower in her remodeled exhibit.**

cling around something else. There's mud in the middle of the yard. A lovely, cool, gooey, giant puddle of mud. It's a ready-made rhino wallow.

Wild Sumatran rhinos love mud. Wallowing in mud keeps them cool and soothes their sensitive skin. The gooey dirt protects them from sunburn and biting bugs. But Andalas has never lived in the wild. And Emi hasn't seen a real mud wallow in many years. Will these zoo rhinos take to the mud? No one has to wonder for long. Emi quickly lowers herself down into the deliciously cool mud. Ahhh. Her son soon follows. "They're in it every day," says Paul. It's the Sumatrans' summer home. The only thing that lures Andalas out of the wallow is food. Especially birthday cake.

At the end of the summer, Andalas's birthday arrives. The not-so-little one-year-old rhino now weighs nearly 900 pounds (408 kilograms). If a human baby grew that much, it'd weigh more than 100 pounds (45 kilograms) by age one. "So how's the birthday boy doing, Terri?" asks Katie Couric, co-host of television's *Today Show*. The Cincinnati Zoo is holding a big celebration in honor of its world-famous rhino baby, including a birthday party on live morning television.

"Andalas is just fabulous," Terri tells the television camera. The scientist glances over at the birthday boy rhino standing in the dusty exhibit yard and smiles. "He pretty much stole our

**Bottom: Emi and Andalas take a lovely mud bath in their wallow.**

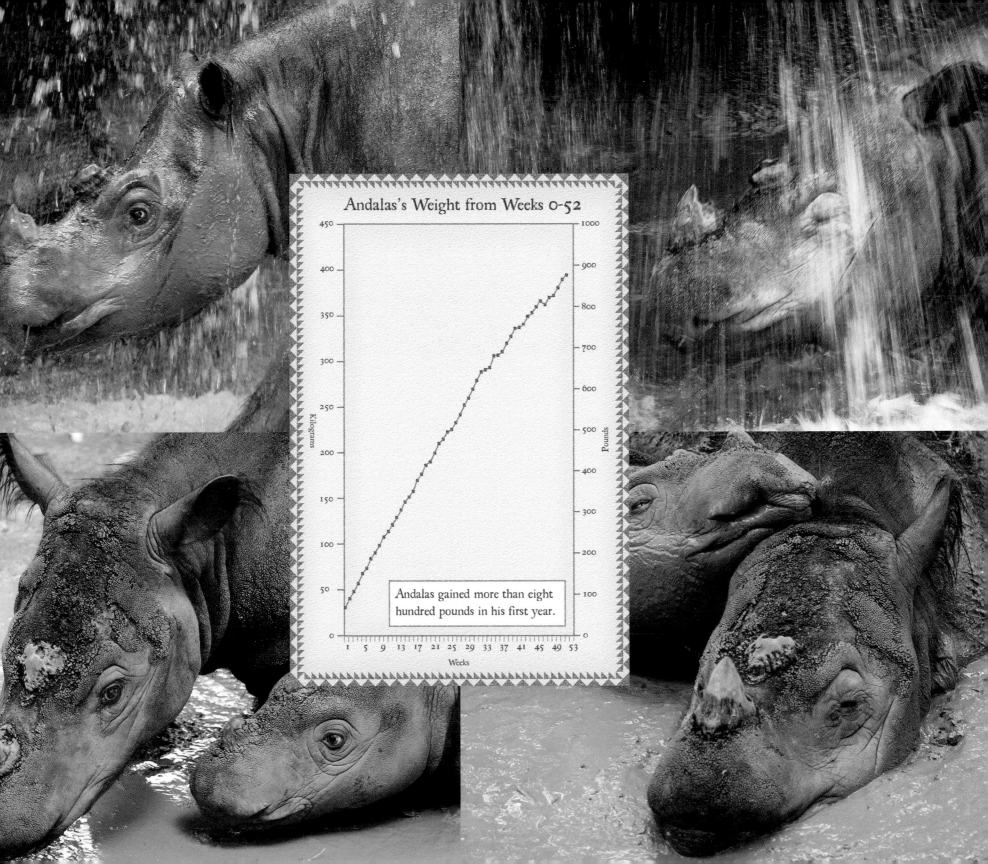

## Andalas's Weight from Weeks 0-52

Kilograms

Pounds

Weeks

Andalas gained more than eight hundred pounds in his first year.

**Andalas (on the right) shares his banana-frosted bread bowl "birthday cake" with mom Emi.**

hearts the day he was born." As cameras send his picture around the world, Andalas concentrates on his cake. His special birthday cake is a big bread bowl stuffed with apples and sweet potatoes. It's frosted with mashed bananas and has a carrot for the candle. Yum!

## Emi's Encore

As Andalas grows bigger, his play with Emi gets rowdier. "He hooks his nose under her flank and lifts her off the ground," says Terri. Emi has gotten rougher with her son, too. It's all part of learning to be a tough male rhino, but it also

means it's time for Andalas to move out of Emi's stall. The "teenaged" rhino needs his space. With Andalas now on his own, everyone hopes Emi would get pregnant for a second successful time. Terri decides it's time to mate the famous rhino couple again. More than two and a half years have passed since Ipuh and Emi were last together. Emi greets Ipuh like an old friend, running circles around him in the yard. Older Ipuh can't quite keep up. Still, he happily rubs heads and horns with Emi. The proud parents successfully breed.

With Emi pregnant again, Terri Roth

has a big decision to make. The last time Emi was pregnant, Terri gave her a progesterone supplement used with horses. Will Emi lose this pregnancy if she doesn't take the hormone supplement again? Terri suspects that Emi might not need it now that she's successfully had a calf. "With Emi having gone through an entire pregnancy," explains Terri, "whatever was out of whack with her system before might be okay now." Besides, even if the supplement helped Emi have Andalas, Terri's not exactly sure how it helped. "I don't even know if the supplement plays the same role in the rhino as it does in the horse," admits Terri. "I may not figure that out in my lifetime—not with rhinos." Unlike with horses, there are very few rhinos in breeding programs. There's only so much scientists can know.

Another reason Terri wants to skip the supplement is to make a point. Terri wants to prove that Sumatran rhinos can breed in captivity naturally, without hormones. "I want to give Emi a chance to carry a pregnancy by herself," says Terri. But only one chance. If Emi loses this pregnancy, they'll feed her hormone-soaked stacks of bread the next time.

Stacks of bread are never ordered. Emi stays pregnant without any hormone help. Weeks turn into months—with Emi still holding on to her pregnancy. Terri's sonograms show a healthy calf growing inside Emi. And supermom Emi is doing it all by herself. It's taken some high-tech science to discover how Sumatrans reproduce. Terri's discovery that these unique hairy rhinos are induced ovulators solved the mystery of Emi's cycle. Terri can now time the matings to the exact twenty-four-hour window when Emi can get pregnant, thanks to the sonograms and blood work research. "But all the research was just to get the species to breed naturally as safely as possible," says Terri. Success!

## Departures and Arrivals

Everyone waits with excitement during Emi's sixteen-month natural pregnancy. Now that

**Terri feeds supermom Emi some apple treats. She's earned them!**

baby number two is on the way, the Cincinnati Zoo needs more room for rhinos. "So we moved Andalas to his mom's old zoo," says Terri. He's given a hero's welcome at the Los Angeles Zoo. Andalas adores his new keepers, especially Steve Romo, his dad Ipuh's old keeper who's now at the L.A. Zoo. They rub and pet him and feed him banana treats. The young rhino's new vet says he looks like a hairy red dinosaur.

Even though Andalas is now a Californian, CREW scientists still track and study his growth. They hope that information about how fast Andalas is growing will help scien-

**Andalas heads for the shade at the Los Angeles Zoo. The five-year-old rhino weighs in at just over 1,500 pounds (680 kilograms).**

tists learn the age when male Sumatran rhinos are ready to breed. "He'll probably be mature in maybe two to three more years," says Terri. "Males mature slower."

By steamy July, Emi is once again huge, moody, and restless. She paces in her stall, rubs her horns on the bars, and urinates a lot. On July 30, 2004, the waiting ends. Emi gives birth to a healthy seventy-five-pound (thirty-four-kilogram) daughter! Supermom Emi becomes the first captive Sumatran rhino *ever* to have two calves. "It's proof the science of breeding Sumatran rhinos has been developed at the Cincinnati Zoo," said Terri. "And that the first birth was not a one-time wonder." Emi's daughter is pretty special, too. The bottom half of her right front leg is white. The birthmark makes it look as if she's wearing one knee sock.

When Emi and her little daughter parade out for their first public appearance, the rhino yard seems extra shady. The zoo added a sun-blocking canopy over the Sumatran rhino exhibits. Wild Sumatran rhinos live in dark forests. Too much sun can damage their eyes. Terri measured the light in a Malaysian forest to find out just how dark the rhino's exhibit should be to build the protective sunshade. "The shade filters out 90 percent of the UVB," says Terri. Ultraviolet B (UVB) light is the dangerous part of sunlight, the part that causes sunburn and skin cancer. Emi, Ipuh, and their

Emi's daughter, Suci, has a birthmark. The bottom half of her right front leg is white instead of red-brown.

**Terri tests the strength of the sunlight under the Sumatrans' sunshade with a light meter.**

daughter are now safer in their shadier exhibit.

The spunky girl calf is named Suci (SUE-chee). It means "sacred" in Indonesian. It's a perfect name. "Sumatran rhinos are on the brink of extinction," says Terri. "Every calf serves as a lifeline for a species clinging so desperately to survival." Terri laughs when she talks about the differences between the two calves. Andalas liked to be petted and rubbed from the start, but Suci is feisty and fussier. "I just think Andalas is more like his mother," explains Terri. "And Suci is more like her father." They're quite a family—a royal rhino family.

**Emi and Suci share a meal in their indoor stall.**

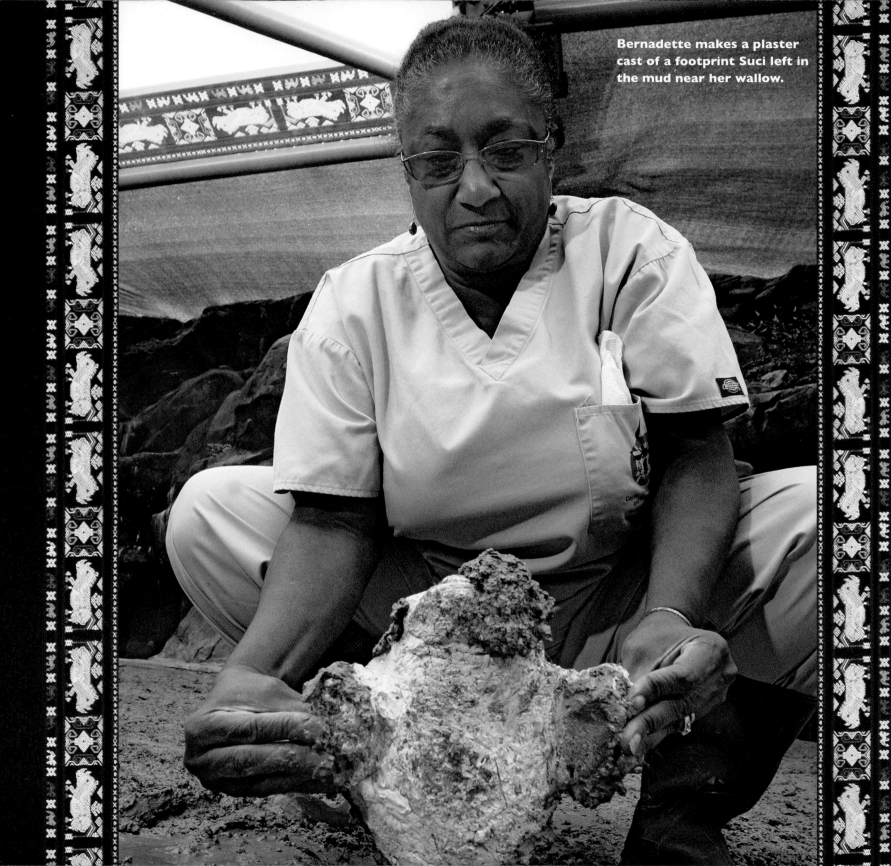

Bernadette makes a plaster cast of a footprint Suci left in the mud near her wallow.

# HELP FOR WILD RHINOS

The rhino yard is quiet at the Cincinnati Zoo. No rhinos wallow in mud or nibble on branches. Emi, Ipuh, and Suci are inside for now. No khaki-clad zookeepers are out cleaning the yard, either. There's just one person crouched down near the rhinos' wallow. It's CREW scientist Bernadette Plair. With both hands, she carefully pulls something out of the mud. It looks like a dirty grayish rock, but it's really a chunk of dried plaster. Bernadette has just made a cast of young Suci's foot. "The footprint in the mud makes the mold for me," says Bernadette. She copies the footprint by making a plaster cast.

Bernadette looks over her collection of footprint casts from Suci. Scientists are using measurements from the casts to estimate the ages of young rhinos that have left footprints in the forests of Indonesia.

The CREW scientist has been making copies of Sumatran footprints since Suci's big brother, Andalas, was born. Why? "In the wild, Sumatran rhinos are solitary forest dwellers," says Terri Roth. "They are rarely seen by humans." Those that study them in the wild often see only what the rhinos leave behind—wallows, dung, and footprints. When wildlife scientists spotted small footprints, they could only guess at the age of the young rhinos that made them. Bernadette's footprint project changed that. Now footprints in the wild can be matched with measurements from Andalas's and Suci's footprints at different ages.

Park rangers and wildlife scientists are already using the footprint measurements from Emi's calves to identify the age of young Sumatran rhinos in the wild. "This is a great example of how captive animals can help their wild counterparts," says Terri. Nearly everything that CREW has discovered about Sumatran rhinos helps their wild relatives. Knowing how they reproduce, what they eat, and how quickly they grow helps wildlife scientists better understand what these rare rhinos need to survive in the wild—as well as better care for them in captivity.

All captive rhinos—not just Sumatrans—help out their wild cousins. Many rhinos are part of important research and breeding programs. And all zoo rhinos teach people about these amazing ancient animals. Visitors who see these giant horned creatures often learn about the deep trouble rhinos are in around the world. Some will care enough to give money to help protect wild rhinos. Others will travel to see wild rhinos themselves. Spending money to see wild animals, like rhinos, can help to protect them. Tourist dollars often pay for rangers and help keep parklands protected.

Many CREW scientists and keepers at the Cincinnati Zoo have traveled to see the kinds of animals they work with in the wild. Emi's

**Above: Emi greets her fans with muddy style. The Sumatran rhino exhibit at the Cincinnati Zoo is popular with visitors young and old.**

**Below: Tourists on East African safari go out of their way to spot black rhinos like this one in Tanzania.**

zookeeper Paul Reinhart has seen both black and white wild rhinos in Africa and recently visited Sumatra. "There's nothing like seeing a wild rhino," he says. Watching a wild rhino move through tall grass, its long horn stretching toward the blue sky, is an amazing sight. "It really makes you want to do more," says Paul. "And get across to people that these animals need attention."

## Going the Distance to Save Rare Rhinos

Terri Roth heads into the jungle. She's on the Indonesian island of Sumatra, where Emi was born about fifteen years ago. Special park rangers called rhino protection units (RPUs) go with Terri into the green shady forest. In the tangle of trees and ferns lives a female Sumatran rhino, who has been showing up along roads and in villages. The young rhino doesn't seem afraid of people. The RPU rangers have named the friendly rhino Rosa.

Terri has heard about Rosa and wants to meet the odd rhino for herself. When the group finds Rosa in the forest, she doesn't run. Instead she comes up to greet each person, as a family pet would. The young rhino is around three and a half years old—near Andalas's age. Her friendliness reminds Terri of Emi, too. Terri slowly reaches out her hand. The CREW scientist brushes her fingers across the rhino's big rough-skinned nose. Terri Roth has traveled around the world, and seeing other kinds of wild rhinos isn't new to her. She's

been up close and personal with many captive Sumatran rhinos. "But Rosa's the only truly wild Sumatran rhino I've seen," says Terri.

Terri Roth didn't travel thousands of miles to Indonesia just to meet Rosa. She's there to help those working in Sumatra with their captive rhino breeding program. Breeding captive rhinos is important, because captive-bred rhinos like Andalas and Suci are part of a backup population for their species. Rhinos in this backup population can sometimes go back to the wild, too. Black rhinos were moved from zoos to a national park in South Africa in 2002. The once-captive rhinos have now had two calves in the wild. There are more rhino reintroduction plans like these in the works for both captive white and black rhinos.

**Terri took this picture of Rosa in the forests of Sumatra, Indonesia.**

**Rhino protection units (RPUs) like this one patrol forests in both Malaysia and Indonesia. RPU rangers look for poachers and destroy wildlife traps and snares.**

Captive rhinos can be released only where it's safe, and safety is a problem for Sumatran rhinos. Poachers have killed so many. Only three hundred or so remaining Sumatran rhinos live scattered in the shrinking patches of uncut forest. "You go through a lot of trouble and years of effort to try to breed these animals in captivity," explains Terri. No one's going to put Sumatran rhinos back into the wild unless they're safe from poachers. That's the job of the RPUs.

RPU rangers patrol the tropical forest home of Sumatran rhinos in both Indonesia and Malaysia. Poachers catch Sumatran rhinos using traps and snares. RPU rangers comb the forest on foot, following trails created by rhinos. They destroy any traps or snares they find. The RPUs also keep a count, or census, of the rhinos in their area. Sometimes RPU rangers

rescue a trapped rhino—or a too friendly one such as Rosa.

Wandering into villages isn't safe for a rhino. It would be easy for a poacher to kill Rosa. The RPU rangers have been keeping an eye on her, but they can't watch Rosa all the time. Not long after Terri met Rosa, wildlife rangers and scientists decided the rhino would be safer in captivity. They captured Rosa and eventually moved her to the Sumatran Rhino Sanctuary in Way Kambas National Park. Rosa is now happily settled into her new, safe home.

## The Future of Earth's Smallest Rhinos

Rosa will hopefully be part of the rhino breeding program at Way Kambas once she's older. Terri Roth will likely see the friendly rhino again, as

# Way Kambas National Park

she works with the sanctuary's staff, traveling to Sumatra regularly. Terri has learned a lot about Sumatran rhino reproduction from Emi, Ipuh, Andalas, and Suci. She hopes that knowledge can help the Sumatran Rhino Sanctuary someday successfully breed rhinos, too. Breeding captured rhinos in their home countries would be easier than shipping them to the United States. Unfortunately, Emi is the only captive Sumatran rhino mom so far.

Sumatran rhinos are critically endangered animals, but no one at the Sumatran Rhino Sanctuary or CREW thinks they're doomed. These hairy rhinos can be saved from extinction. Protecting rhino habitat and battling poachers has helped black, Indian, and white rhinos in recent years. Sumatran rhinos will also survive if their forests are preserved and made safe. No one wants to think of a world without its smallest and hairiest rhino.

Andalas himself is going to help out. "The plan is to send Andalas to Sumatra," says Terri. Emi's first calf will move to the Sumatran Rhino Sanctuary and join their breeding program someday soon. When he goes, Andalas will step onto the same forested island his mother left years ago. The sights, smells, and sounds will seem new to Andalas. But he'll be home for the first time.

## What's Everyone Up to Now?

**Emi and other rhinos at the Cincinnati Zoo paint pictures using their flexible upper lips. Money from selling the paintings goes to the International Rhino Foundation to help their wild rhino cousins.**

Emi, Ipuh, and Suci are all still living at the Cincinnati Zoo. When this book went to press, Emi was again pregnant, with her third calf.

Andalas was sent to Sumatra in February of 2007. The hope is that there he'll breed with one of the captured female rhinos, possibly Rosa.

You can get an update on Emi and her family at www.cincinnatizoo.org/ Conservation/GlobalConservation/ SumatranRhino/sumatranrhino.html.

Watch what Emi is up to on the RhinoCam at www.aroundcinci.com/ icams/rhino/.

For updates on Rosa and the other rhinos at the Sumatran Rhino Sanctuary, visit www.rhinos-irf.org/irfprograms/ asiaprograms/sumatranrhinobreeding centers/waykambassrs/index.htm.

# BLACK RHINO

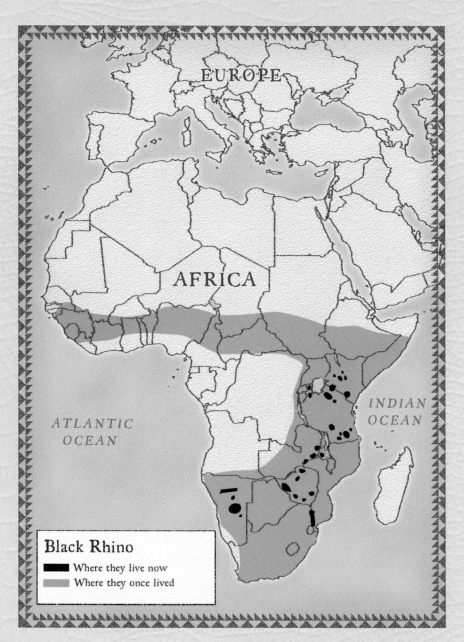

**Black Rhino**
- ■ Where they live now
- ▨ Where they once lived

**SCIENTIFIC NAME:**
Diceros bicornis

**OTHER NAMES:**
hook-lipped rhino,
prehensile-lipped rhino

**RANGE:**
eastern and southern Africa

**HABITAT:**
tropical bushlands and grasslands

**FOOD:**
leafy plants, shrubs, and tree leaves
and branches

**HEIGHT:**
4.5–5.5 feet (1.4–1.7 meters)

**LENGTH:**
10–12.5 feet (3–3.8 meters)

**WEIGHT:**
1,750–3,000 pounds
(794–1,361 kilograms)

**HORN:**
two horns, the front one much
longer and curving back

**HOW MANY?**
3,600 in the wild and 250 in captivity

## Black Rhino Facts

- Black rhinos aren't black. Their hide is grayish brown and often covered with a layer of dried mud or dust. Their dark covering of dirt earned them the name "black" rhino.

- Black rhinos are smaller than the other kind of African rhino, the white rhino. Black rhinos are fast-moving and can run as fast as thirty miles (forty-five kilometers) per hour.

- Black rhinos are browsers. This means they don't graze on grass like a cow. Instead, they eat leaves and twigs off bushes and trees, more like a deer.

- Black rhinos have a grasping, or prehensile, hook-shaped upper lip. Their prehensile upper lip easily strips leaves and twigs off branches.

- The black rhino's long front horn can grow to 3.5 feet (1.1 meters) long. Black rhinos use their horns to defend themselves and as a tool to dig up tasty bushes and small trees.

- Black rhinos are usually solitary and live alone. A calf lives with its mom for two and a half to three years.

- Black rhinos almost went extinct during the 1970s and 1980s when poachers killed more than 60,000 of them. Thanks to protection, today their numbers are slowly increasing, though much of Africa is no longer home to black rhinos.

# White Rhino Facts

- White rhinos aren't white. The name came from *weit*, the Afrikaans word for "wide" (mouth). Their smooth hide is a grayish color.

- White rhinos are grass-chomping grazers. Their wide bottom lip hugs the ground like a lawn mower.

- The heads of white rhinos hang low and close to the ground. White rhinos can't pick their heads up very high. In fact, they can drown in water deeper than their nose.

- White rhinos are social animals. About a dozen females, calves, and young rhinos live together in a small herd. Male, or bull, rhinos live alone.

- White rhinos can live to be fifty years old.

- White rhinos are today the least threatened rhino. Conservationists in South Africa protect their rhinos from poachers. They've also moved white rhinos back into areas where they once lived. This has helped the population grow to more than 11,000.

**SCIENTIFIC NAME:**
*Cerathotherium simum*

**OTHER NAME:**
square-lipped rhino

**RANGE:**
southern and central Africa

**HABITAT:**
savannah grasslands

**FOOD:**
grass

**HEIGHT:**
5–6 feet (1.5–1.8 meters)

**LENGTH:**
12.5–15 feet (3.8–4.6 meters)

**WEIGHT:**
4,000–6,000 pounds
(1,814–2,722 kilograms)

**HORN:**
two horns, the front one is larger

**HOW MANY?**
11,300 in the wild and 750 in captivity

# WHITE RHINO

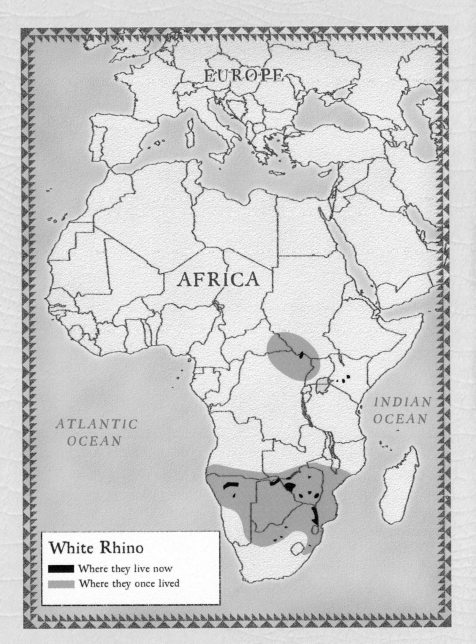

EUROPE

AFRICA

ATLANTIC OCEAN

INDIAN OCEAN

**White Rhino**
▬ Where they live now
▬ Where they once lived

# INDIAN RHINO

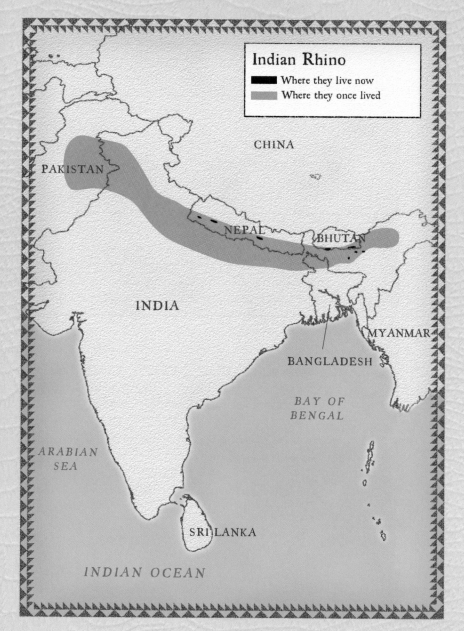

Indian Rhino
- ■ Where they live now
- ▨ Where they once lived

CHINA

PAKISTAN

NEPAL

BHUTAN

INDIA

MYANMAR

BANGLADESH

BAY OF
BENGAL

ARABIAN
SEA

SRI LANKA

INDIAN OCEAN

**SCIENTIFIC NAME:**
*Rhinoceros unicornis*

**OTHER NAMES:**
Asian greater one-horned rhino,
Nepalese rhino

**RANGE:**
northern India and southern Nepal

**HABITAT:**
grasslands along rivers

**FOOD:**
grass and water plants

**HEIGHT:**
5.75–6.5 feet (1.75–2 meters)

**LENGTH:**
10–12.5 feet (3–3.8 meters)

**WEIGHT:**
4,000–6,000 pounds
(1,814–2,722 kilograms)

**HORN:**
one horn

**HOW MANY?**
2,500 in the wild and 150 in captivity

## Indian Rhino Facts

- Indian rhinos are brownish gray. Their bumpy skin hangs in folds that look like plates of armor.

- Male Indian rhinos have a large skin fold below the throat. It's called a bib.

- Indian rhinos are the largest rhinos. Only elephants are bigger land animals.

- The upper lip of Indian rhinos is somewhat prehensile, or grasping. It helps them browse on bushes as well as graze grass.

- Indian rhinos are usually solitary, except for moms with calves.

- They poop in giant dung heaps that can be three feet (one meter) high and fifteen feet (five meters) across.

- Indian rhinos are good swimmers and like to spend time in the water. They'll even sink down into deep water to eat underwater plants.

- In the early 1900s only 200 Indian rhinos were left in Asia. Thanks to protection in India and Nepal, these giant rhinos have increased to more than 2,000 living in the wild.

# Javan Rhino Facts

- Javan rhinos have armor-like skin folds and one horn, like Indian rhinos, but are smaller. This is why Javan rhinos are also called Asian *lesser* one-horned rhinos.

- Javan rhinos browse on leaves, twigs, and branches in their forest homes. They are solitary, living alone.

- Javan rhinos once lived in the forests all over Southeast Asia—Thailand, Laos, Vietnam, Malaysia, Myanmar, and Indonesia. Today only two tiny populations remain. One is in Vietnam and another on the Indonesian island of Java. All are in protected parks.

- Scientists thought Javan rhinos were extinct everywhere except Java until 1988 when a small group was discovered in Vietnam.

- With only sixty left, Javan rhinos are the rarest rhinos on Earth. The remaining Javans are well protected in parks and aren't disappearing as fast as Sumatran rhinos, which are considered more endangered.

**SCIENTIFIC NAME:**
*Rhinoceros sondaicus*

**OTHER NAME:**
Asian lesser one-horned rhino

**RANGE:**
Java and Vietnam

**HABITAT:**
tropical rain forest

**FOOD:**
leaves, twigs, and plants

**HEIGHT:**
5–5.5 feet (1.5–1.7 meters)

**LENGTH:**
6–11.5 feet (1.8–3.5 meters)

**WEIGHT:**
2,000–5,000 pounds
(907–2,268 kilograms)

**HORN:**
one small horn; some females have none

**HOW MANY?**
60 in the wild and none in captivity

# JAVAN RHINO

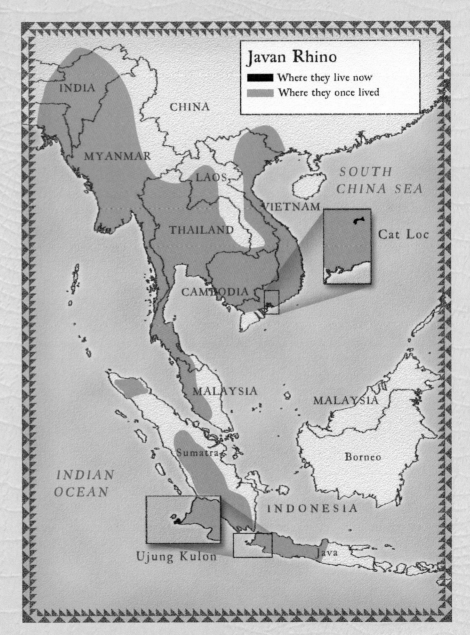

Javan Rhino
- Where they live now
- Where they once lived

# SUMATRAN RHINO

Sumatran Rhino

■ Where they live now
■ Where they once lived
? Unconfirmed sighting

INDIA

CHINA

MYANMAR  LAOS

SOUTH CHINA SEA

THAILAND

VIETNAM

CAMBODIA

MALAYSIA

MALAYSIA

Borneo

INDIAN OCEAN

Sumatra

INDONESIA

Java

**SCIENTIFIC NAME:**
*Dicerorhinus sumatrensis*

**OTHER NAMES:**
Asian two-horned rhino, hairy rhino

**RANGE:**
Sumatra, Borneo, and Malay Peninsula

**HABITAT:**
thick tropical forest

**FOOD:**
leaves, shrubs, twigs, fruit, and other plants

**HEIGHT:**
3–5 feet (1–1.5 meters)

**LENGTH:**
6.5–9.5 feet (2–2.9 meters)

**WEIGHT:**
1,300–2,000 pounds (590–907 kilograms)

**HORN:**
two horns, the front larger and the back horn very stubby

**HOW MANY?**
300 in the wild and 10 in captivity

## Sumatran Rhino Facts

• Emi, Ipuh, Andalas, and Suci are Sumatran rhinos. Emi is the only Sumatran rhino ever to give birth to two calves in captivity.

• The brown skin of Sumatran rhinos is covered in shaggy red-brown hair. Other kinds of rhinos have only a bit of hair around their eyes, ears, and tails.

• Sumatrans are the smallest rhinos. They're half the size of Indian rhinos.

• Sumatrans are the only Asian rhino with two horns. Their horns are small.

• They eat all kinds of fruit, leaves, twigs, and bark in their tropical rain forest home.

• Sumatrans move quickly through dense forest and are hard to spot in the wild.

• They are solitary animals, except for females with calves.

• Sumatran rhinos like to wallow in mud. They also travel to natural salt licks during full moons.

• Sumatran rhinos once lived in much of Indonesia, Malaysia, and parts of Southeast Asia. Today only 300 Sumatran rhinos survive on the islands of Sumatra and Borneo and the Malay Peninsula.

• Over the past fifteen years, poachers have killed more than half the world's Sumatran rhinos. This fast decline makes them the most endangered rhino on earth.

# Words to Know

**anesthetize**
to give a drug that causes unconsciousness or prevents feeling.

**artificial insemination (AI)**
creating pregnancy by injecting sperm into the womb.

**browsers**
animals that eat leaves, twigs, and buds.

**cast**
an object made from a mold.

**conservationists**
people who preserve, manage, and care for the environment.

**critically endangered**
facing an extremely high risk of extinction in the wild.

**data**
information, like facts or numbers, from experiments or observations.

**dung**
the feces, or poop, of a large animal.

**ecosystem**
a system made up of a group of living things, their environment, and the relationships between them.

**embryo**
a tiny, undeveloped unborn animal.

**endangered**
in danger of becoming extinct.

**exhibit**
the place a zoo animal can be seen by the public.

**extinct**
died out; no longer existing or living.

**grazers**
animals that eat grasses.

**habitat**
the place where an animal or plant naturally lives.

**herbivores**
animals that eat plants.

**hormones**
chemicals that control and regulate body functions.

**induced ovulator**
a female animal that ovulates only when mated.

**keratin**
a tough, stringy substance that makes up hair, nails, feathers, hooves, and rhinoceros horns.

**mammal**
a warm-blooded animal with fur or hair that gives birth to live young that nurse their mother's milk.

**miscarriage**
the separation of a fetus from its mother's womb before it can survive on its own.

**ovulation**
the ripening and release of an egg or eggs from the ovary.

**poachers**
hunters that illegally kill or collect animals or plants.

**population**
the number of individual animals or plants of a particular species.

**progesterone**
a female hormone important in reproduction.

**range**
the place where a particular species of animal or plant naturally lives.

**reintroduction**
the returning of captive animals back into the wild.

**scientific method**
the process of gaining knowledge by collecting facts through observation and experiments to answer a question or prove a prediction.

**sonogram**
an image created with sound vibrations, often of the inside of someone's body; also called an ultrasound.

**species**
a category of living things made up of related individuals able to produce offspring that can themselves reproduce.

**supplement**
something that supplies what is needed by a living thing, like a vitamin, nutrient, or dose of hormone.

**threatened**
not currently endangered but still threatened with extinction or likely to be endangered in the near future.

**ultraviolet B**
light that can cause sunburn and cell damage.

# Learn More About Rhinos

### Web Sites

Visit these Web sites for up-to-date rhino information:

- **International Rhino Foundation:** www.rhinos-irf.org
- **SOS Rhino:** www.sosrhino.org
- **Asian Rhino Project:** www.asianrhinos.org.au
- **Rhino Resource Center:** www.rhinoresource center.com

Listen to rhino voices at www.thewildones.org/Conflict/rhino.html.

### Books

Cunningham, Carol, and Joel Berger. *Horn of Darkness: Rhinos on the Edge* (Oxford University Press, 2000).

Toon, Steve, and Ann Toon. *Rhinos: Natural History and Conservation* (Voyageur Press, 2002).

### How to Help Rhinos

- Buying this book will help rhinos. A portion of the royalties from this book will be donated to the Cincinnati Zoo Rhino Conservation Fund (www.cincinnatizoo.org).
- Take part in the International Rhino Foundation's North American Save the Rhinos campaign. This campaign will aid the three most critically endangered rhino species—Sumatran, black, and Indian rhinos—by protecting their wild habitat and supporting captive breeding (www.rhinos-irf.org).

# Photo credits

4 - Top left photo of young Terri Roth (from Terri Roth)

6 - Painting of woolly rhino (Marcus Jackson)

9 - Rhino icons on map (Marcus Jackson)

14 - Terri Roth with snares (from Terri Roth)

21 - Rhinos mating (Dave Jenike)

24 - Three photos of baby Andalas (Dave Jenike)

25 - Newborn Andalas and inset Terri Roth (Dave Jenike)

37 - Top row, second from left (Dave Jenike); bottom far right (Dave Jenike)

40 - Andalas's birthday (Dave Jenike)

47 - Rosa (Terri Roth)

48 - RPUs (Terri Roth)

53 - Javan rhino (Alain Compost)

All other photos by Tom Uhlman.

# Acknowledgments

I am infinitely grateful to Dr. Terri L. Roth, vice president of Conservation, Science & Living Collections at the Cincinnati Zoo and Botanical Garden and director of the Center for Conservation and Research of Endangered Wildlife (CREW). Her research and discoveries helped Emi become a mother and give hope to endangered species conservationists across the globe. I'm personally thankful to Terri Roth for taking the time to tell me the story of Emi and her family, patiently explain her research, and pose for photos, as well as review the manuscript. Thanks also to CREW reproductive physiologist Monica Stoops and CREW research associate Bernadette Plair for sharing their work, data, and time. I'm also grateful to Paul Reinhart, team leader of the Ungulate Department, and all the other rhino keepers at the Cincinnati Zoo who care for these magnificent creatures and allowed myself and photographer Tom Uhlman repeated access to them. Thanks as well to Lynn Blattman, Marcus Jackson, Dave Jenike, Barb Rish, and Chad Yelton of the Cincinnati Zoo and Botanical Garden for their spirited help with press materials and images. I'd also like to thank Steve Romo and the Los Angeles Zoo for their help. I'm grateful as well to the late Tom Foose, program director of the International Rhino Foundation, for his kind assistance. Special thanks to my editor, Erica Zappy, whose enthusiasm for Emi's story allowed an idea to become this book.

# Index